getting CRAFTY
DUCT TAPE

DANA MEACHEN RAU

45TH PARALLEL PRESS

Published in the United States of America by Cherry Lake Publishing Group
Ann Arbor, Michigan
www.cherrylakepublishing.com

Reading Adviser: Beth Walker Gambro, MS, Ed., Reading Consultant, Yorkville, IL
Illustrator: Ashley Dugan
Book Designer: Felicia Macheske

Photo Credits: © SashaMagic/Shutterstock, 4; NASA/Eugene A. Cernan, public domain, via
Wikimedia Commons, 6: © Madlen /Shutterstock, 7

45th Parallel Press is an imprint of Cherry Lake Publishing Group.

Library of Congress Cataloging-in-Publication Data

Names: Rau, Dana Meachen, 1971- author. | Dugan, Ashley, illustrator.
Title: Duct tape / written by Dana Meachen Rau ; illustrated by Ashley Dugan.
Description: Ann Arbor, Michigan : Cherry Lake Publishing, [2023] | Series: Getting crafty |
    Audience: Grades 4-6 | Summary: "Explore your creative side and get crafty with duct
    tape! Discover new skills and learn the many creative uses of duct tape, from making
    reversible belts to pencil cases to stadium seats and more! Book includes an introduction
    on what duct tape is and the history behind the invention. It also includes several projects
    with easy-to-follow step-by-step instructions and illustrations. Book is developed to aid
    struggling and reluctant readers with engaging content, carefully chosen vocabulary, and
    simple sentences. Includes table of contents, glossary, index, sidebars, and author
    biographies"—Provided by publisher.
Identifiers: LCCN 2022041802 | ISBN 9781668919583 (hardcover) |
    ISBN 9781668920602 (paperback) | ISBN 9781668923269 (pdf) |
    ISBN 9781668921937 (ebook)
Subjects: LCSH: Tape craft—Juvenile literature. | Duct tape—Juvenile literature.
Classification: LCC TT869.7 .R383 2023 | DDC 745.5—dc23/eng/20220902
LC record available at https://lccn.loc.gov/2022041802

Cherry Lake Publishing Group would like to acknowledge the work of the Partnership for
21st Century Learning, a Network of Battelle for Kids. Please visit *http://www.battelleforkids.
org/networks/p21* for more information.

Printed in the United States of America
Corporate Graphics

TABLE OF CONTENTS

IDEAS THAT STICK!

Are you full of ideas? Are you creative? Creative people are good at lots of things. Creative people are **resourceful**. That means they find new ways to solve problems. They invent useful objects. Sometimes they do this by using an item for a different job than it was intended.

Duct tape was created to help people seal and fix things. But you can use it for other things! Think of other ways to use duct tape. You can turn it into objects you can use. You can use duct tape to decorate objects. Use things you already have!

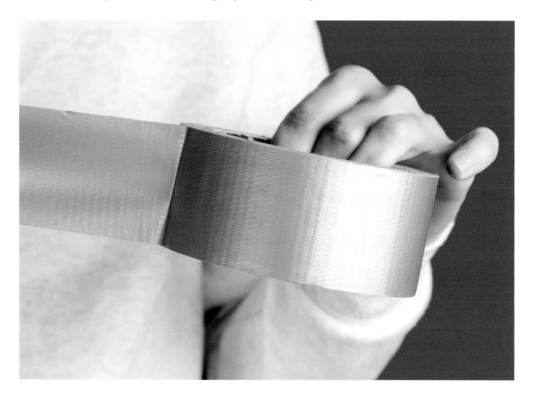

Duct tape is a **pressure-sensitive adhesive**. That means force is needed to make it stick. But just a little bit. When you lay duct tape on a surface, you just need to swipe it with your hand to make a strong bond.

What ideas do you have for turning a roll of duct tape into something new?

The THREE LAYERS of DUCT TAPE

- The top layer is a **flexible** plastic coating. This means it bends. It makes the tape waterproof.

- The middle layer is cotton fabric. This makes the tape strong. It make it easy to cut or tear.

- The bottom layer is a sticky glue. It's made of rubber. It can stick to most surfaces.

FIX-IT TAPE

During World War II (1939–1945), soldiers needed a way to keep their things dry. They needed a tape that was strong and waterproof. Duct tape was perfect. Soldiers found lots of uses for this tape, including fixing equipment and making bandages.

After the war, people found lots of other uses for duct tape. They could repair almost anything, indoors or out! Today, many people keep duct tape in their toolboxes or kitchen drawers. Astronauts even bring duct tape into space.

The tape used in the war was green. The tape today is often gray. But duct tape comes in a rainbow of colors. It comes in a rainbow of patterns!

BASIC TOOLS

You need duct tape to make the projects in this book! You will also need other tools and materials.

DUCT TAPE

Duct tape comes in rolls. You can make a project with just one color of duct tape. Do you want to make stripes or other designs? Buy a few rolls in different colors and patterns. Duct tape is about 2 inches (5 centimeters) wide.

CUTTING TOOLS

Duct tape is made of fabric. That means you can rip it into smaller pieces. But you will need scissors or a craft knife to get a clean edge. Craft knives are sharp! Always ask an adult for help when you use one. If you use a craft knife, you also need a cutting mat.

WORK SURFACES

For some projects, you will need to lay the tape sticky side down. But you don't want it to stick to your work surface! Tape peels up easily from a cutting mat. No cutting mat? You can cover your work surface with wax paper. Tape the wax paper down with painter's tape.

YARDSTICK, RULER, AND TAPE MEASURE

You need tools to help you measure your tape. A yardstick is good for long measurements. A ruler works for shorter ones. Use a tape measure to measure around an object.

BE CAREFUL!
Try not to get duct tape stuck on yourself. It can hurt when you pull it off your skin.
YOWCH!

MAKING FABRIC STRIPS and SHEETS

Depending on your project, you may need strips of duct tape. You might need sheets of duct tape. This is like fabric. It has tape on both sides. It can then be made into bags, wallets, cell phone cases . . . Anything else you can imagine.

MAKE A TWO-SIDED STRIP

1. Cut two strips of duct tape the same length.

2. Lay one strip on your work surface, sticky side up.

3. Place the center of the other piece, sticky side down, on top of the first piece. Start by just touching the centers together. Line them up. Short pieces are easy. Longer pieces are harder.

4. Lay each side down. Work slowly and carefully. Working with a partner can make this easier. Flatten from the center to the ends with your hands. Push out air bubbles. You now have a two-sided strip of fabric.

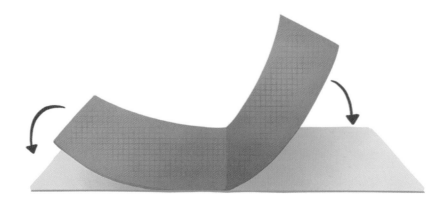

MAKE A HANDLE

1. Cut two strips of duct tape. One of them should be about 2 inches (5 cm) shorter than the other.

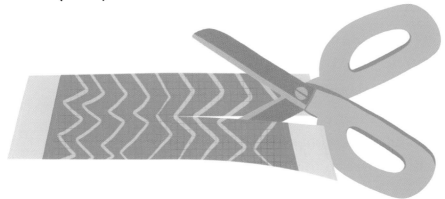

2. Lay the longer strip on your work surface, sticky side up. Place the center of the shorter piece, sticky side down, on top of the first. The sticky side of the bottom strip will extend about 1 inch (2.5 cm) on each end.

3. Cut the strip in half the long way.

4. Fold the center of each strip in half the long way. Be careful with the sticky ends. Now you have two handles. Simply attach the sticky ends to anything that needs handles!

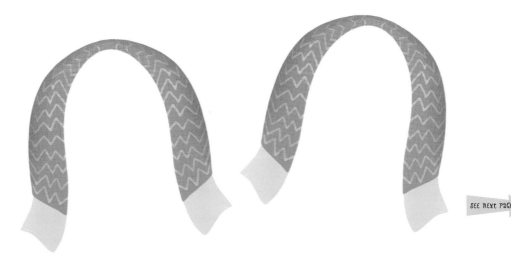

SEE NEXT PAGE

MAKE A TWO-SIDED SHEET OF FABRIC

1. Lay a strip of duct tape on your surface. Sticky side up. Lay a strip sticky side down. Overlap the first about 1 inch (2.5 cm).

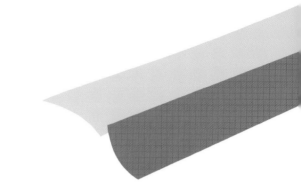

2. Flip your sheet of fabric over. Add on another strip. It should overlap the one above a little bit.

3. Flip it over again. Lay down another strip.

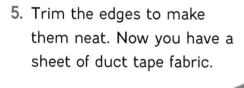

4. Continue flipping, adding strips until you have the size you want.

5. Trim the edges to make them neat. Now you have a sheet of duct tape fabric.

MAKING TABS

Tabs are small pieces of duct tape. Half is fabric. Half is sticky. You can use them to make flaps or fringe. You can use them to make other details for creations.

MAKE A SQUARE FLAP

1. Cut a piece of duct tape. Make it about 6 inches (15 cm) long.

2. Fold over 2 inches (5 cm) of the tape from one end. Stick it to itself. Press it flat. Now part of the strip is fabric. Part of it is sticky.

MAKE FRINGE

1. Make a square flap.

2. Use scissors to cut slots into the fabric side. Start at the folded edge.

MAKE A TRIANGLE FLAP

1. Cut a piece of duct tape. Make it about 3 inches (7.6 cm) long.

2. Fold one corner to the center. Fold the other corner to the center. Press flat. Now you have 1 inch (2.5 cm) of triangle fabric. You have 2 inches (5 cm) of sticky surface.

3. Here's another way to make a triangle. Fold the bottom edge over to a side edge. Then you'll have 2 inches (5 cm) of triangle fabric. You'll have 1 inch (2.5 cm) of sticky surface.

FRINGE FLOWERS

Everyone loves getting flowers! Flowers are good to decorate with too! Practice your duct tape tab-making skills. Create a flower! Make it colorful!

MATERIALS
- Unsharpened pencil
- Green duct tape
- 2 other solid colors of duct tape (color **A** and color **B**)
- Ruler
- Scissors

STEPS

1. Make six fringe tabs for each flower (see page 13), three with color **A** and three with color **B**.

2. Place the end of the pencil on a color **A** tab. Roll it around the pencil. Press to seal.

3. Place that wrapped pencil on a color **B** tab, lining up the fringe ends. Roll it around the pencil. Press to seal.

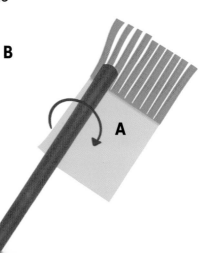

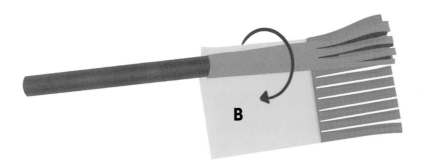

4. Continue adding the rest of the fringe tabs. Alternate color **A** and color **B**.

5. Make two triangle tabs with the green duct tape.

6. Roll one of the green tabs around the pencil. Press to seal. Repeat with the other green tab.

7. Fold down the green "leaves."

8. Fold back the fringe "petals" one or two at a time. Beautiful!

A COLORFUL MEAL

Are you in charge of setting the table for dinner? Bring some color! Bring some creativity! Bring some colorful duct tape place mats!

MATERIALS

- 3 colors/patterns of duct tape (colors **A**, **B**, and **C**)
- Ruler
- Scissors

STEPS

1. Make five 15-inch (38 cm) two-sided strips of color **A**. Make six 10-inch (25 cm) two-sided strips of color **B** (see page 10).

2. Cut an 8-inch (20 cm) strip of color **C**. Lay it sticky side up on the work surface. Place the ends of the color **A** strips along the color **C** strip, overlapping about 1 inch (2.5 cm).

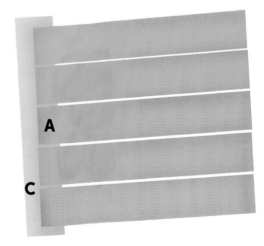

3. Weave a color **B** strip over and under the color **A** strips as shown. To weave, start by placing the color **B** strip beneath the first color **A** strip. Place it on top of the next color **A** strip. Alternate between placing the color **B** strip under and on top of the color **A** strips.

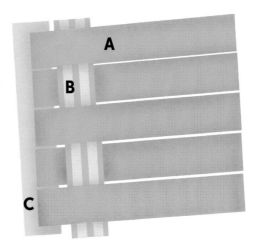

4. Weave a second strip of color **B** in the opposite way you wove the first strip. If you started under color **A** for the first strip, start on top of color **A** for this strip. Continue weaving the rest of the color **B** strips until you reach the end.

5. Fold over the color **C** strip on the end to help hold all of the strips in place. Trim the ends.

6. If needed, trim the edges on the other three sides so that all the strips are even.

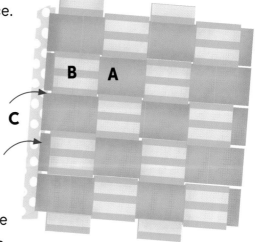

7. Lay a strip of color **C** on the opposite edge, overlapping about 1 inch (2.5 cm). Fold over and trim the edges. Then lay strips along the top and bottom. Fold over and trim.

JAZZY JARS

Jazz up an old jar or glass. Make a vase for flowers. Make a pencil holder. It can hold whatever you like! Try different color combos. Give your vase a wild look!

MATERIALS

- A jar or glass
- 2 colors/patterns of duct tape (color **A** and color **B**)
- Ruler
- Scissors

STEPS

1. Make a bunch of square tabs (see page 13). The amount you need will depend on the size of your jar. Cut the square tabs in half. Make them into rectangular tabs.

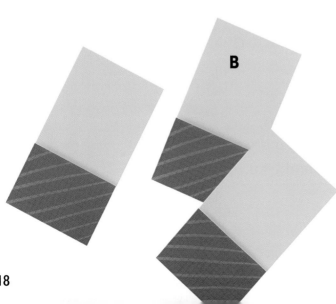

2. Start at the bottom of the jar. Stick the tabs around the jar. Alternate color **A** and color **B**. The tabs should extend about .25 inch (0.6 cm) beyond the bottom of the jar.

3. Add a second row of tabs above the first. Alternate the pattern so that color **A** sits above color **B**.

4. Add a third row. Add a fourth row. Add as many as you need to reach the top of the jar. When you get to the last row, fold the sticky parts of the tabs over the top of the jar.

5. Turn the jar upside down. Fold the tabs downward so they poke out. Then flip the jar right side up.

REVERSIBLE BELT

A duct tape project you can wear! Belts are a cool addition to any outfit. By using two patterns of duct tape, you can wear the belt two ways. You'll have two belts in one!

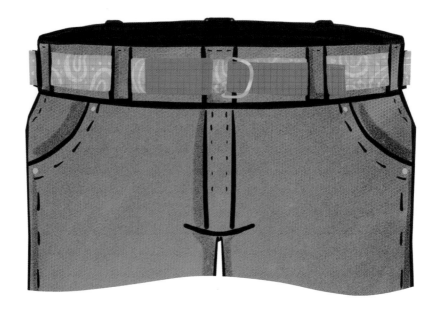

MATERIALS

- 2 patterns of duct tape (pattern **A** and pattern **B**)
- Scissors
- Tape measure
- Yardstick
- 2 D-ring belt fasteners (buy these at a craft or fabric store—or remove them from an old belt)

STEPS

1. Measure your waist. Use a tape measure. Add about 6 inches (15 cm). Use this measurement to cut a strip of pattern **A** and pattern **B**.

2. Stick these strips together. Make a two-sided strip (see page 10). These pieces are long. They will be hard to line up perfectly. But you will be cutting the strip later. You don't have to be too perfect.

3. Cut the two-sided strip to fit inside your belt rings.

4. Thread the end of the two-sided strip into both rings. Fold over the end about 2 inches (5 cm). Tape it down with a piece of duct tape.

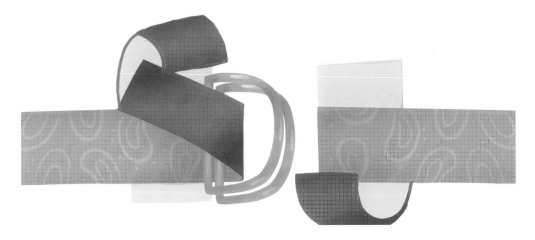

5. Add a piece of duct tape to the other end of the strip, too. This will make it stronger.

6. To wear the belt, insert the strip through both rings. Thread the end back through one ring. Pull to tighten.

PENCIL CASE

Go to school in style! Bring a cool, custom pencil case. Use it to hold all your supplies.

MATERIALS

- 8-inch (20 cm) zipper (buy this at a craft or fabric store)
- Duct tape
- Ruler
- Scissors

STEPS

1. Tape the ends of the zipper. Use small pieces of duct tape. Place a strip of duct tape about 10 inches (25 cm) wide along one side of the zipper.

2. Flip it over.

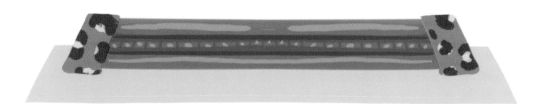

3. Lay another piece of duct tape over the first to start your fabric (see page 12).

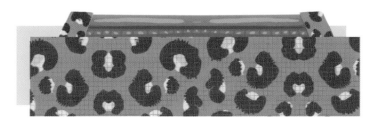

4. Flip the strip over to the front. Make fabric until it measures about 5 inches (12.7 cm) long. Fold over the bottom sticky edge. Or trim it.

5. Repeat steps 1 to 3 on the other side of the zipper.

6. Trim both side edges so they are even.

7. Fold down the sides of the case. The zipper will be at the top. Tape the bottom edges closed. Use strips of duct tape. Trim the ends.

8. Close the two sides. Use strips of duct tape. Trim the ends.

CHEER-UP TISSUE BOX

Got a runny nose? Or a scratchy cough? Decorate a box of tissues! Use fun, cheery colors. Brighten up your next sick day! Or share with a friend who's feeling sad.

MATERIALS

- Tissue box
- 2 colors/patterns of duct tape (color **A** and color **B**)
- Scissors
- Craft knife

STEPS

1. Unfold the box of tissues. Don't rip it where it is glued. Remove the tissues. Set them aside. Don't pull them apart. Lay the box out flat.

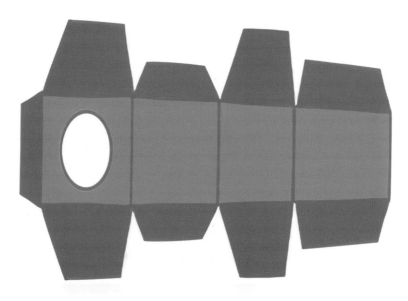

2. Cut strips of duct tape. Make them longer than your box. Lay a strip of color **A** across the middle. Then, slightly overlapping each strip, alternate color **A** and color **B**. Completely cover the box.

3. Trim the duct tape from the areas between the outer flaps. Fold over the extra tape on the ends. Cut out the hole for the tissues. Use a craft knife.

4. Refold the box along its original folds. Place the tissues back inside. Seal the flaps closed with duct tape.

A USEFUL BOX

Out of tissues? Put the box on your desk. It can hold pens, pencils, or other small items. Or you could use it to display your duct tape flowers!

SOFT STADIUM SEAT

Woo-hoo! It's fun to cheer on your team. But sitting in bleachers can get uncomfortable. Bring this comfy seat to your next event. Decorate it with your team's colors. Show your support!

MATERIALS

- Bubble wrap
- 2 colors/patterns of duct tape (color **A** and color **B**)
- Ruler
- Scissors

STEPS

1. Fold or stack pieces of bubble wrap. Make a square about 16 inches (41 cm) on each side. Make it about 2 inches (5 cm) thick. Tape it together with small pieces of duct tape.

2. Cut a strip of color **A**. Make it a little wider than the bubble wrap "pillow." Tape it across the center of the pillow.

3. Lay strips of color **A** above and below the middle strip. Overlap them a little. Cover the whole surface.

4. Trim the edges even. Fold them over onto the edges of the cushion. (It's okay if the edges are a little rough. You'll cover them later.)

SEE NEXT PAGE

5. Flip the cushion over. Repeat steps 2 to 4 on this side.

6. Cut a strip of color **B**. Make it a little wider than the pillow. Lay it across the bottom edge. Fold it over. Close the opening. Repeat on the top. Trim the edges.

7. Cover the sides with strips of color **B**. Trim the edges.

8. Make two handles with color **B** (see page 11). Make them about 12 inches (30 cm) long.

9. Stick the handles along the top edge. Cover the base of each handle with color **A**.

COVER IT UP!

You can make colorful duct tape creations for all parts of your day. Start the morning using a toothbrush with a colorful handle. Cover a notebook to use at school. Decorate a lunch box with stripes of patterned tape. Make a wallet to hold your allowance. Make a bouquet of fringed flowers. The ideas are endless! What can you come up with?!

GLOSSARY

flexible (FLEK-suh-buhl) able to bend

pressure-sensitive adhesive (PREH-shuhr SEHN-suh-tiv ad-HEE-siv) a substance, such as glue, that makes things stick together with a little bit of pressure

resourceful (rih-SOHRS-fuhl) able to solve problems in creative ways

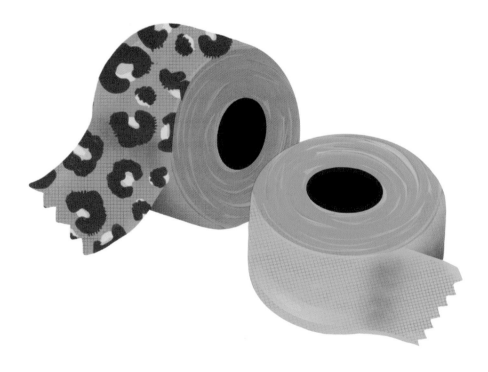

FOR MORE INFORMATION

BOOKS

Bell-Rehwoldt, Sheri. *The Kids' Guide to Duct Tape Projects*. Mankato, MN: Capstone Press, 2012.

Dobson, Jolie. *The Duct Tape Book*. Richmond Hill, ON, Can: Firefly Books, 2012.

Morgan, Richela Fabian. *Tape It and Make It: 101 Duct Tape Activities*. Hauppauge, NY: Barron's, 2012.

Wallenfang, Patti. *Just Duct Tape It!* Little Rock, AR: Leisure Arts, 2011.

INDEX